MARION LÉVY AND VÉRONIQUE GEORGE
CONCEIVED BY PAULINE RICARD-ANDRÉ

SCREEN YOUR STUFF

A Fun, Funky Introduction to Silk-Screening
Your Tees, Totes, Towels, and More

Photography by Coco Amardeil

Watson-Guptill Publications / New York

*/ CONTENTS

THE QUEENS OF SCREEN

MARION LÉVY and **VÉRONIQUE GEORGELIN** met at the School of Decorative Arts in Paris. After finishing school, they met again at the Peclers Style Agency in Paris and began working together, designing collections for other people. Both were fascinated by **SILK SCREEN PRINTING** and the strong, luscious colors it can produce. After fifteen years of intense activity, the two launched their own line of silk-screen printed fabrics, under the name Maisongeorgette.

Maisongeorgette fabrics—some still printed by hand—mix and layer simple, bold design elements, such as **GIANT POLKA DOTS**, showers of confetti, Japanese flowers, and fireworks. Randomly placed designs and joyful displays of color are their trademarks.

Marion and Véronique still find constant joy in the **ART AND CRAFT** of silk screen printing, from the meditative motion of spreading ink through the screen to the magic of seeing a printed design for the first time. They wish you the same delight, whether this is your first time trying silk screen printing—or your five hundredth!

FINDING INSPIRATION

At Maisongeorgette, we find inspiration in anything and everything, whether designed, printed, painted, or silk screened. Pictures, illustrations, **GRAFFITI**, flowered kimonos, **VINTAGE FABRICS**—joyful mixtures of color and strong graphic design define the Maisongeorgette style. In our studio, vast numbers of pots filled with colored inks are evidence of our constant search for new color harmonies. Pencils and paper are our rough materials, as every one of our ideas begins life as a **SKETCH** on paper.

*⁄ OUR SECRET COLOR RECIPES

⫽⫽⫽ We use Pébéo's transparent Setacolor fabric paints, available online and in most craft stores, because we love their transparent hues. By mixing them with Setacolor Lightening Medium, we make them less opaque without thinning the paint. Here are some of the recipes we use to get intense, eye-popping colors. It's fine to use other fabric paints and dilutants, but you'll have to tinker with the recipes accordingly, and the colors will vary somewhat. Mix the paints in old glass jars with lids to close them. Glass jam jars work well as they're reusable and will keep for a long time.

We recommend mixing a range of varying tones. Here are recipes for 2 dark colors (black and plum), 2 neutral colors (beige and rich brown), 1 grayish tint (light blue), 1 bright color (red), and 2 super-bright colors (fluorescent pink and orange). Follow the recipes carefully. The quantities given are enough to make any project in this book.

*18

LIGHT BLUE

8 tablespoons Setacolor Lightening Medium
½ teaspoon Turquoise #30
2 drops Red Ochre #20
2 drops Bright Orange #21
2 drops Lemon Yellow #17
2 drops Velvet Brown #14

 ## FLUORESCENT PINK

5 tablespoons Setacolor Lightening Medium
1 ¼ teaspoons Fluorescent Pink #33
½ teaspoon Lemon Yellow #17

 ## FIERY RED

5 tablespoons Setacolor Lightening Medium
2 teaspoons Bright Orange #21
2 teaspoons Vermillion #26

PLUM

4 tablespoons Setacolor Lightening Medium
6 teaspoons Plum #01
¼ teaspoon Cobalt Blue #11

 ## BEIGE

7 tablespoons Setacolor Lightening Medium
5 drops Fuchsia #49
10 drops Lemon Yellow #17
5 drops Velvet Brown #14
3 drops Cobalt Blue #11

RICH BROWN

9 tablespoons Setacolor Lightening Medium
¼ teaspoon Velvet Brown #14
¼ teaspoon Lemon Yellow #17
¼ teaspoon Lawn Green #04
10 drops Fuchsia #49

 ## ORANGE

4 tablespoons Setacolor Lightening Medium
1 teaspoon Bright Orange #21
¼ teaspoon Lemon Yellow #17
2 drops Lawn Green #04

BLACK

3 tablespoons Setacolor Lightening Medium
3 tablespoons Black Lake #19

CHOOSING COLORS

These are some of our favorite color combinations. Try pairing very different colors to find harmonies that are interesting and surprising.

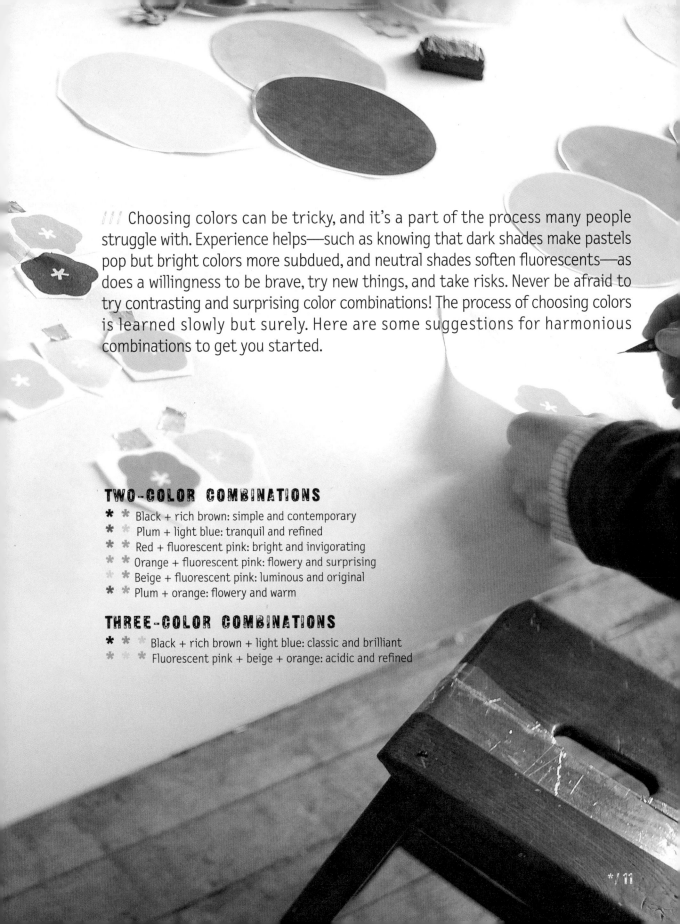

/// Choosing colors can be tricky, and it's a part of the process many people struggle with. Experience helps—such as knowing that dark shades make pastels pop but bright colors more subdued, and neutral shades soften fluorescents—as does a willingness to be brave, try new things, and take risks. Never be afraid to try contrasting and surprising color combinations! The process of choosing colors is learned slowly but surely. Here are some suggestions for harmonious combinations to get you started.

TWO-COLOR COMBINATIONS

* * Black + rich brown: simple and contemporary
* * Plum + light blue: tranquil and refined
* * Red + fluorescent pink: bright and invigorating
* * Orange + fluorescent pink: flowery and surprising
* * Beige + fluorescent pink: luminous and original
* * Plum + orange: flowery and warm

THREE-COLOR COMBINATIONS

* * * Black + rich brown + light blue: classic and brilliant
* * * Fluorescent pink + beige + orange: acidic and refined

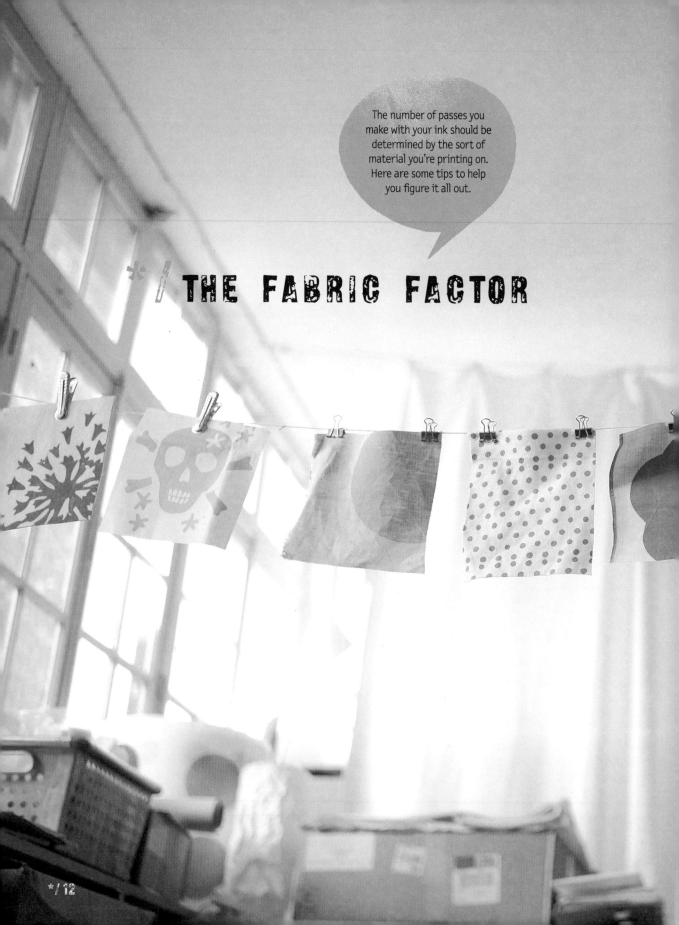

The number of passes you make with your ink should be determined by the sort of material you're printing on. Here are some tips to help you figure it all out.

*1 THE FABRIC FACTOR

Almost any kind of material can be silk screened—fabric, paper, cardboard, even oilcloth—as long as it has a smooth surface. Avoid silk screening leather or velvet, whether smooth or corded, as the ink will stay on the surface and the material will become as stiff as cardboard. The important thing is to adjust the number of times you pass ink through the screen for your particular fabric—more passes for thicker fabric, fewer for thinner materials. (See the cheat sheet below for our recommendations.) Once the colors have been fixed with a hot iron, all printed materials except oilcloth can be machine-washed at 104°F (40°C).

MATERIALS CHEAT SHEET

ORGANDY, FINE CLOTH (COTTON, LINEN, OR SILK), NONWOVEN MATERIALS, PAPER, AND CARDBOARD
1 pass, there and back

CANVAS (COARSE, SILK, OR LINEN), JERSEY (T-SHIRTS), DENIM
2 passes, there and back

WOOL FELT, TWEED, BLANKET
3 passes, there and back

OILCLOTH (USE SÉTACOLOR OPAQUE PAINT FOR THIS)
1 pass, there and back

*TOOLS OF THE TRADE

MAKING A FRAME AND STENCIL

/// This is a simplified version of professional silk screen printing. Basically, you cut a stencil out of self-adhesive screen-printing film (or clear acetate), or buy a pre-made stencil. (The *cut-out* part of your stencil is what gets printed on the fabric.) You then adhere your stencil to the polyester mesh of a silk-screen frame, available in any crafts store. The frame can be reused as many times as you wish.

Depending on the complexity of your design, it can take anywhere from 20 to 50 minutes to apply a stencil to the frame.

1 / Cut out a rectangular piece of self-adhesive screen-printing film about ½ inch (1cm) smaller (on all sides) than the screen inside the frame.

2 / Draw or photocopy your design, or trace a template from the back of this book. Tape your design to a window and tape the piece of screen-printing film on top. Trace your design onto the film.

3 / Use a craft knife to carefully cut out the *inside* of the design, leaving the rectangle intact.

4 / Cut out the details (hearts, petals, and so on) and set them aside.

5 / Carefully stick the rectangle of film onto the mesh screen.

6 / Check that the film has stuck firmly, smoothing it to remove any bubbles.

7 / Stick the cut-out details onto the screen, using your traced drawing as a guide.

8 / Use wide tape to mask any screen not covered by the film, to keep ink from passing through it to your fabric.

9 / Let the frame dry for at least an hour before use.

WHAT YOU NEED

* FRAME STRETCHED WITH POLYESTER MESH SCREEN, BOUGHT FROM A CRAFTS STORE (CHOOSE ONE A LITTLE LARGER THAN THE DESIGN YOU WANT TO SCREEN PRINT)

* ROLL OF ADHESIVE SCREEN-PRINTING FILM (TRANSPARENT OR OPAQUE)

* CRAFT KNIFE

* CUTTING BOARD

* PENCIL

* SCISSORS

* ROLL OF WIDE ADHESIVE TAPE (FOR MASKING)

*/10 STEPS TO PRINTED MAGIC

/// Anything can be printed as long as it meets two conditions: first, it must be able to lie completely flat, without any protruding items such as zippers, buttons, buckles, and so on. (Many of these things can, of course, be removed and sewn back on after printing.) And second, it cannot be shaped, like baskets or your sunhat.

1 / Start by prepping your workspace. Cover it with a piece of felt or an old towel first, then a clean cloth on top, securing both with tape so they don't move around. If you're printing a small design, an ironing board is probably large enough. Put on an apron. Iron the fabric to be printed, then secure it to the table or ironing board with straight pins. Have the prepared frame ready, as well as a squeegee, a jar of paint or ink, and a scrap of fabric to do a trial run.

2 / Do the trial run first. Place the frame over your practice fabric.

3 / Pour about 3 tablespoons of ink evenly along the upper edge of the screen, avoiding the stencil area.

4 / Hold the frame firmly on the table with one hand. With your other hand, pull the squeegee toward you, exerting light pressure and dragging the ink evenly down to the bottom of the frame. The squeegee should be held at a 45-degree angle, as shown below left.

5 / Now go back in the opposite direction, pushing the ink with the squeegee. The ink should always stay in front of the squeegee. The process is easier with two people—one to hold the frame in place, the other to pull and push the squeegee.

6 / Carefully remove the screen from the fabric. Check if your practice run was successful before starting on your actual fabric.

7 / Place the frame carefully on your fabric and repeat steps 3–5. The thicker the fabric, the more passes you should make back and forth with the squeegee (see pages 12-13 for tips on printing various materials).

8 / Carefully lift the frame. To repeat the design, move the frame to a different spot and do steps 3–5 again. If you want to print the same design on different items (T-shirts, pillowcases, and so on) there is no need to wash the frame and wait for it to dry. Simply prepare the items in advance, pin them down flat, and print them. (If you want to use a different color, however, you'll have to wash and dry the screen first, as in step 9.)

9 / When you're done, use a spatula to collect excess paint on the frame and put it back in the ink jar. Rinse the frame in a shower or sink. (Be sure to rinse out the shower immediately afterward, so the color doesn't dye your bathroom!) Once it is completely dry, the screen can be used again with a different color.

10 / Dry your printed fabric with a hairdryer on full power, making sure the dryer never touches the fabric. To fix the design permanently, press it with a hot iron for two minutes. The printed fabric can then be machine-washed at 104°F (40°C).

WHAT YOU NEED

* LARGE PIECE OF FELT OR OLD TOWEL
* LARGE PIECE OF CLEAN MATERIAL TO COVER THE TOWEL
* STRAIGHT PINS
* APRON OR OLD SHIRT
* EMPTY GLASS JARS WITH LIDS
* TABLESPOON FOR EACH COLOR
* SQUEEGEE (AVAILABLE AT CRAFTS STORES)
* SPATULA
* HAIRDRYER

*/ QUICK FIXES FOR ANNOYING PROBLEMS

orgette

THE OUTLINE OF YOUR DESIGN IS BLURRY

/// You may have moved the frame while printing, and ink ran under the screen. Print the design several times on scrap fabric to clear the screen, then try the print again.

THE DESIGN IS SMUDGED

/// Part of your stencil has come unstuck from the screen. Wash and dry the frame, then reapply the stencil and let it dry for a longer period this time. If worst comes to worst, you may have to make a new stencil.

SMALL PARTS OF YOUR STENCIL—LIKE HEARTS AND PETALS—HAVE COME UNSTUCK

/// Re-cut the pieces out of fresh adhesive film and stick them back onto the well-dried screen. Let dry thoroughly before trying to print again.

THE COLOR IN YOUR PRINTED DESIGN IS UNEVEN

/// It could be one of three things: you didn't put enough pressure on the squeegee, you didn't do enough passes with the ink, and/or you didn't use enough ink. Try again, increasing the pressure, the number of passes, or the amount of ink accordingly.

YOU'RE TIRED OF DEALING WITH STENCIL PROBLEMS

/// If you are one of those people who want to avoid all stenciling problems, do what professionals do—apply your stencil photographically to the screen. (See page 63 for a list of sources.)

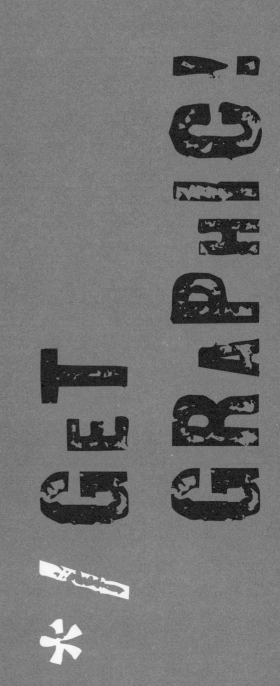

*/ GET
GRAPHIC!

These are some of our favorite 2-color combinations:
plum + light blue
fiery red + light blue
orange + beige
fluorescent pink + beige.
Why not make one cushion of each?

*/ DOTTY CUSHIONS

UPDATE YOUR CUSHIONS WITH GIANT POLKADOT COVERS

/// These cushion covers are made from cream-colored felt, which is easy to work with because its raw edges need no hemming. Use them to cover a pillow form, or any old pillow that needs updating. The appeal here is in the way the huge dots are randomly placed. Or try layering them for unexpected color combinations. (See page 57 for dot template.)

1/ Measure your cushion and add 1 inch (2.5cm) to each side. Use a pencil to lightly draw this outline on a piece of felt.

2/ Prepare your colors. Decide where you want the dots. Print the light-colored dots first. Let dry, then print the dark-colored ones.

3/ Cut out the cover (you can cut through some of the printed dots). Cut out a plain piece of felt for the back, the same height as the cushion front but 6 inches (15cm) wider. Cut this piece in half down the center. Sew the backing pieces to the cover, overlapping them in the back to form an envelope opening, then slip your pillow inside.

*/24

We love this weird juxtaposition of cheery red dots and take-no-prisoners skull and crossbones.

*/ TO-DIE-FOR TOTE

GIVE YOUR MESSENGER BAG SOME EXTRA MUSCLE

/// Before printing the bag, make sure there are no patches, zippers, buckles, or bulky seams where the design is to be printed. If there are, either re-position the design or remove the patch, buckle, or zipper. (See page 57 for dot template, page 60 for skull and crossbones.)

1/ Prepare red and plum colors for the dots, black for the skull and crossbones.

2/ Pin the flap down flat and flatten out the bag.

3/ Print the red dots. Let dry. Print the plum dot, let dry again.

4/ Center the skull and crossbones design and print it in black. Let dry.

We recommend placing your design high and in the center: around 2 ½ inches (6cm) from the neckline for a child's tee and 4 inches (10cm) for an adult's.

*⁄ GRAPHIC TEES

GET PERSONAL WITH YOUR CLOTHES

⁄⁄⁄ Give design pride of place on your T-shirt—whether a template from pages 56-61, or your own by-you-for-you stencil.

For "true" color, print on a white T-shirt. If printing on a colored tee, the color of the print will be affected by the background color. The paler the T-shirt, the more luminous the printed color.

If the fabric is very thin, insert a sheet of cardboard inside the T-shirt before printing so the ink doesn't bleed through to the other side.

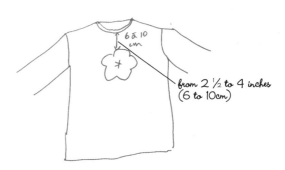

Layer multiple design elements for a fun look, or use one single element for a more powerful statement.

*/ THESE JEANS ROCK

GIVE YOUR FAVORITE BLUES SOME ATTITUDE

/// You know those jeans you've worn a thousand times? Add a personal touch with one graphic element or a riot of design. Place a dot on the back pocket for a knowing wink, put flowers on the knees to evoke the patched jeans of childhood, or print designs all over like a burst of graffiti.

Note that your inks must always be darker than the fabric they are printed on. The lighter the jeans, the stronger the colors will be. On dark jeans it's best to use plum or black. If you want brighter colors, use opaque ink (like the red in the photograph, which is from Pébéo's Sétacolor opaque line) or fabric paint instead.

Finally, make sure the jeans lay as flat as possible for printing.

*/ PEEKABOO WINDOW PANELS

MAJOR IMPACT FOR MINIMAL EFFORT

/// These lightweight panels are made of a nonwoven polyester fabric, so the circular holes need no sewing. Cut 4 panels of nonwoven material, each measuring 43 x 16 inches (110 x 40cm) or whatever length and width you need to fit your windows. (See page 57 for dot template.)

1/ Prepare a range of 3 colors per panel. Here are 3 suggestions: plum, light blue, and rich brown; plum, orange, and beige; or fluorescent pink, beige, and orange.

2/ Print the dots on the fabric panel(s), including those you intend to cut out. When making several panels, vary the colors and positions of the dots.

3/ When the dots are dry, use a craft knife to cut one dot from each panel.

4/ Finish the panels by folding over a ½-inch (1cm) hem at the top and stapling or taping it down.

5/ Hang the panels using clip-on rings and a cord, or a narrow tension rod, or stick them directly to the window with suction cups or double-sided tape.

> We just love bright pink cotton printed with big, red peonies! Sheer voile is a perfect medium for the bright pink and fiery red combo. On transparent fabrics like this, the colors recede just enough to let light filter through.

*/ JAPANESE-INSPIRED PANELS

DOLL UP YOUR DOORWAY

/// Whether covered with peonies, polka dots, or anything else, these panels are so romantic you'll find a thousand uses for them—to separate off part of a room, to transform a bed, or simply to hang at your windows. (See page 56 for flower template.)

1/ Cut out two bright pink voile panels to the size desired.

2/ Prepare the red color, then print the flowers.

3/ When the flowers are dry, sew a hem all around each panel with a double row of machine stitching. To help the panels hang straight, insert a strip of nonwoven fabric into the hem at the base of each panel.

4/ Sew two little tape loops to the tops and hang them from a thin wire, as shown.

* / SPRINGTIME TABLE LINENS

BETTER THAN A VASE OF FLOWERS...

1 / Cut a length of fine linen cloth to fit your table and as many napkins as you want, each measuring 18 x 18 inches (45 x 45cm). The perfectionists among you will want to hem them; the rest of you will just say that fringed, raw edges are more stylish.

2 / Prepare a range of 5 colors. We used beige, orange, fluorescent pink, plum, and fiery red.

3 / Arrange a repeating pattern on the tablecloth, using the flower templates on pages 56 and 58.

4 / Begin by printing the large peonies, then the large dandelions, and finish with the small peonies.

5 / Print just a single flower on each napkin, or use a pattern of small flowers.

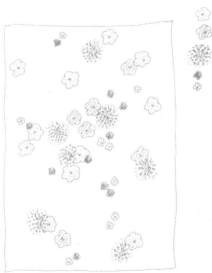

CIRCUS TENT LAMPSHADE

LIGHTEN UP AND GET PLAYFUL

1 / Roll a sheet of paper around your existing lampshade and cut it out to create a pattern. Use the pattern to cut out the same shape in nonwoven flame-retardant fabric.

2 / Decide how many spots you want and what size, then pick colors to match your room, or choose a graphic combo like brown and light blue.

3 / Prepare the colors. Print the light-colored spots first. Let dry, then print the darker-colored ones.

4 / Coat the lampshade with a thin layer of spray adhesive (work in a well-ventilated room and wear a dust mask) and stick the printed fabric onto it.

*⁄ LEFTOVER BEAUTIES

/// After you've printed and created all kinds of beautiful items, use the leftover printed fabric scraps to make these quick, romantic accessories.

Flower market brooch

1 / Using scraps of printed sheer voile and colorful nonwoven material, cut out a variety of stylized flower shapes (see below). Stack them on top of each other, the largest on the bottom.

2 / Secure the stack with a few stitches in the center, then sew a pinback to the back.

Table petals

Follow the directions for the brooch but, to make the flowers more magical, insert shapes cut from metallic gold or silver paper between the layers of fabric. Note: These candles are decorative only and should not be lit.

4³⁄₄ in. (12cm)   4¹⁄₄ in. (11cm)   4¹⁄₄ in. (11cm)   4¹⁄₄ in. (11cm)

4³⁄₄ in. (12cm)   5 in. (13cm)   4 in. (10cm)   3¹⁄₂ in. (9cm)

colored thread

stack, then secure with a stitch in the center

*/ PARTY GARLANDS

FOR ANY DAY YOU FEEL LIKE CELEBRATING, EVEN MONDAY

1 / Cut out irregular circles from scraps of printed voile and nonwoven fabric.

2/ Thread the circles like beads onto a cord with a large-eyed needle, making a knot between each circle to prevent it from sliding along the cord.

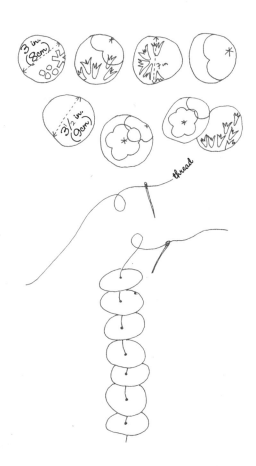

We used flowery colors: fluorescent pink, beige, orange, and plum—layering them here and there to create a vibrant mix.

*1/ LOUNGE LAMPS

/// Follow the instructions on page 37 to cut out your fabric lampshade.

1/ Prepare your colors.

2/ Begin printing with the lighter colors. Let dry. Add the darker colors, overlapping them as desired.

3/ Coat the lampshade with a thin layer of spray adhesive (work in a well-ventilated room and wear a dust mask) and stick the printed fabric onto it.

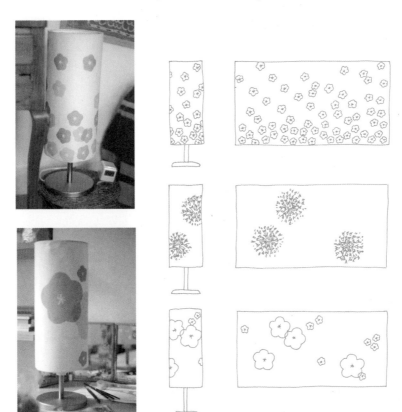

At Maisongeorgette we gravitate toward classic designs and fabrics, but we like to use them in striking, unconventional ways, as in this bedroom.

*⁄ FLOWERFUL BEDROOM

WAKE UP TO A SHOWER OF FLOWERS

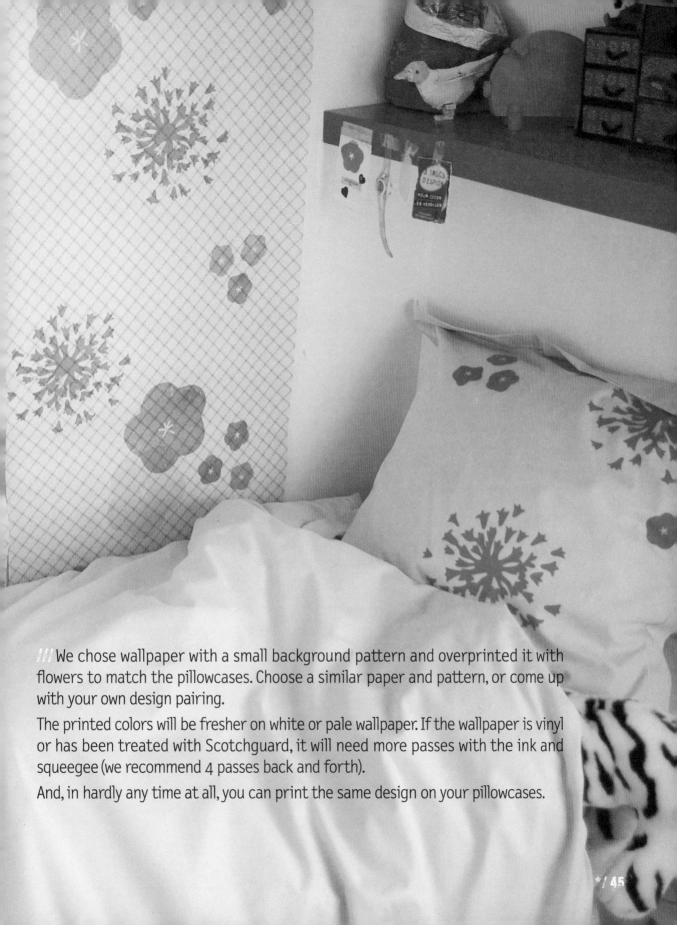

/// We chose wallpaper with a small background pattern and overprinted it with flowers to match the pillowcases. Choose a similar paper and pattern, or come up with your own design pairing.

The printed colors will be fresher on white or pale wallpaper. If the wallpaper is vinyl or has been treated with Scotchguard, it will need more passes with the ink and squeegee (we recommend 4 passes back and forth).

And, in hardly any time at all, you can print the same design on your pillowcases.

*⁄ PUMPED-UP PANTIES

GIVE YOUR UNDIES SOME SELF RESPECT

We chose to use black here,
which felt more "rock'n'roll"
than baby pink.

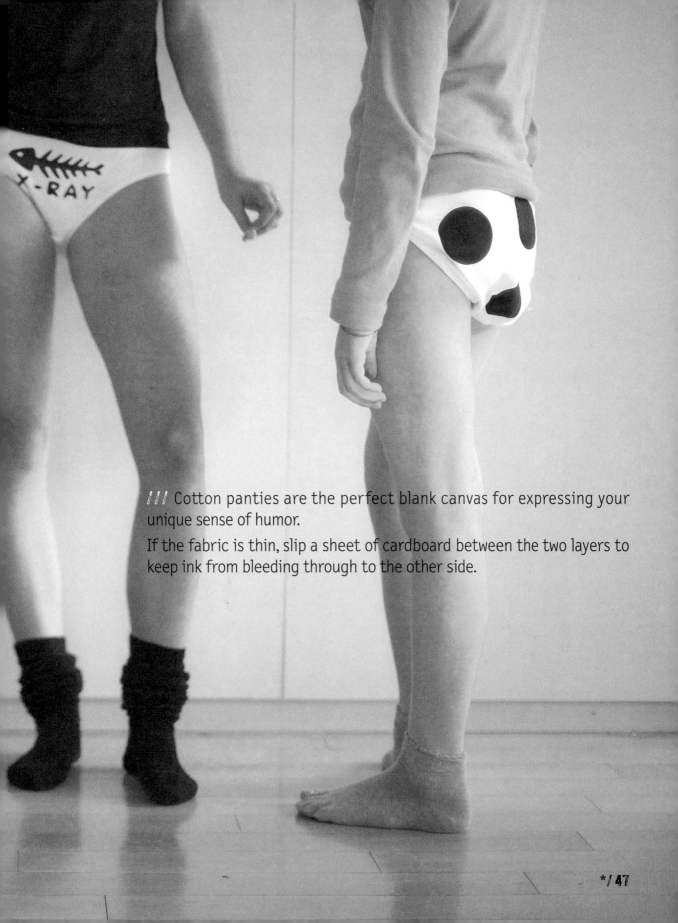

Cotton panties are the perfect blank canvas for expressing your unique sense of humor.

If the fabric is thin, slip a sheet of cardboard between the two layers to keep ink from bleeding through to the other side.

*⁄ SMART-SET DESK SET

/// Brighten up your desk or office with printed storage boxes, notebook covers—even envelopes get the treatment.

To print storage boxes and files, open them up first and lay them flat.

For boxes you can't dismantle, fill them with rigid books so you can hold the frame firmly against the box surface when printing.

Choose studious, attractive color combinations that will go well with brown paper covers. We suggest black and plum, or light blue and fiery red.

...rds and pictures on how to make twinkles ... the eye and colours agree in the dark. Thoughts ... ndscaping, moonlighting and daydream ... you seen a purple cow? When less can be ... n than enough. The art of looking sideways. ... gaze is to think. Are you left-eyed? Living out ... loud. Buy junk, sell antiques. The Golden Mean. ... anding ideas on their heads. To look is to listen. ... Insights on the mind's eye. Every status has its ... symbol. Do androids dream of electric sheep?' ... Why feel blue? Triumphs of imagination such ... as the person you love is 72.8% water. Do not ... adjust your mind, there's a fault in reality. Teach ... yourself ignorance. The belly-button problem. Visual charades. What has an ox to do with the letter A? The art of looking sideways. How to turn knots into bows. When does 1 and 1 add up to 3? Why sit with your back to the view? Notes on the

*⫽ STATIONERY MAGIC

ORDINARY STATIONERY GETS FANCY

⫽⫽⫽ Decorate paper and basic white envelopes with simple, striking designs in fluorescent pink, orange, fiery red, and other bright colors.

To liven up photo albums, travel journals, or recipe books, print your design on nonwoven fabric. Allow the designs to dry thoroughly. Then, using a sewing machine, turn the fabric into a simple cover with flaps into which you can slip the cover of your book or album.

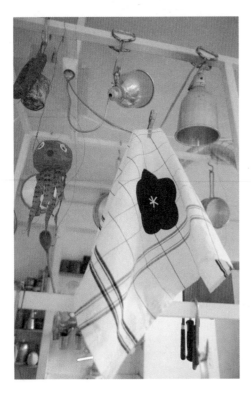

*/ IF YOU CAN DREAM IT, YOU CAN PRINT IT

ONCE YOU START SILK SCREEN PRINTING, YOU WON'T BE ABLE TO STOP!

/// Now that you know the secrets of screen printing, and how easy it is to transform everything in sight, the rest is up to you. Surround yourself with graphic elements and bold color—or go for black or monochromatic prints, as we did here. Create a statement and experience the fun of creating graphic design for yourself!

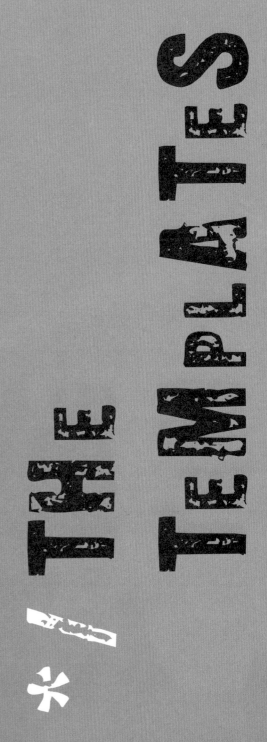

*/ THE TEMPLATES

*/ PEONIES

* DOTS

DANDELION

HEART

SKULL AND CROSSBONES

*/ FISHBONE

X-RAY

*/ RESOURCES

WHERE TO GO FOR WHAT YOU NEED

Check out your local crafts store or art supply store for the silk-screen printing frames, squeegees, screen-printing film, pre-cut stencils, fabric paints, ink, and other supplies and tools. Here are some sources for Pébéo Setacolor fabric paints and photographic mediums as well as general supplies.

PÉBÉO SETACOLOR FABRIC PAINTS AND LIGHTENING MEDIUM, FRAMES FILM, AND OTHER SCREEN-PRINTIN SUPPLIES

Dick Blick Art Materials
www.dickblick.com

Dharma Trading Co.
www.dharmatrading.com

Michaels
www.michaels.com

Pearl Paint
Screen printing supplies but no Setacolor paints.
www.pearlpaint.com

PHOTOGRAPHIC MEDIUMS

DIAZO PHOTO EMULSION
WWW.SPEEDBALLART.COM

PHOTOEZ
WWW.EZSCREENPRINT.COM

ULANO SUPER PREP
WWW.ULANO.COM

OTHER CRAFT STORES

Hobby Lobby
www.hobbylobby.com

Jo Ann Fabric and Craft Stores
www.joann.com

HUGE THANKS TO:

• PÉBÉO for the Setacolor textile paints (www.pebeo.com)
• VÉNILIA for the adhesive film used for the stencils
• TROIS SUISSES for the white T-shirts on page 24, the pillowcases and duvet covers on page 44, and the striped shirt on page 52
• MUJI for the canvas bags on page 25, panties on page 46, apron on page 52, and brown paper notebooks and storage boxes on page 48 (www.muji.fr)
• VITRA for the release of the Eames chair on page 26 (www.vitra.com)
• TSÉ-TSÉ for the Cornette lamp on pages 36 and 40, and the Armlite lamp on page 50
• IKEA for the table lamp on pages 42 and 43 (www.ikea.com)

THANKS TO

Rosemarie Di Domenico, for her confidence and support;
Pauline Ricard-André, for initiating this project and bringing her usual dynamism, implacable good humor, and professional advice;
Coco Amardeil, for her energy and creativity;
Anne Bullat-Piscaglia, for listening so attentively;
Iroko Osawa, for his constant help;
Alice Laroch-Leblanc, for her invaluable helping hands;
Isabel Castel, for the cardboard suitcases;
George Sancho, for his devotion and his parking lot;
and Juliette, Fanny, Rosalie, Samuel and Émile, Jean-Baptiste, and Denis.

First published in the United States in 2008 by
Watson-Guptill Publications
Nielsen Business Media, a division of The Nielsen Company
770 Broadway, New York, NY 10003
www.watsonguptill.com

Library of Congress Control Number: 2007942431

ISBN-10: 0-8230-2476-8
ISBN-13: 978-0-8230-2476-6

First published in France by Marabout (Hachette Livre) in 2006
© Marabout 2006

Designed by Anne Bullat-Piscaglia (voiture14.com)

Printed in Spain by Graficas Estella

1 2 3 4 5 6 7 / 14 13 12 11 10 09 08